Jonah and the Great Big Fish

Rhonda Gowler Greene

Illustrated by Margaret Spengler

ZONDERkidz

For my sons, Matt, Aaron, and Brad, with love.
—RGG

To my sisters, Nancy and Marilyn—for sharing the adventure.
—MS

ZONDERKIDZ

Jonah and the Great Big Fish
Copyright © 2007 by Rhonda Gowler Greene
Illustrations © 2014 by Margaret Spengler

This title is also available as a Zondervan ebook.
Visit www.zondervan.com/ebooks.

Requests for information should be addressed to:

Zonderkidz, 3900 Sparks Dr, Grand Rapids, Michigan 49546

ISBN 978-0-310-73219-8

Editor: Barbara Herndon
Art direction & design: Mary pat Pino

Printed in China

14 15 16 17 18 /LPC/ 10 9 8 7 6 5 4 3 2 1

The word of the Lord came to Jonah ...
"Go to the great city of Nineveh and preach against it,
because its wickedness has come up before me."

Taken from Jonah 1:1–2

God told Jonah to obey,
said, "Go to Nineveh this day.

Preach to all
the people there.
Though they sin,
tell them I care.

Tell them they
need to repent."
Yes, Jonah was the one
God sent.

But, stubborn Jonah fled instead.
Didn't do what God had said.

Yes, he ran
from the Lord.
Saw a ship and climbed aboard.

As he rested
down below,
a mighty wind
began to blow.

Angry waves from the sea
whⁱp_pe^d that ship so violently.
Splashing, crashing waves so tall
made that ship prove weak and small.

The sailors, scared,
but still quite brave,
could not survive that
wind and wave.

Anxious cries,
What to do?
They asked Jonah, "**Who** are you?"

He said, "I fled from the Lord.
Paid my way and climbed aboard."

Jonah added, "Throw me in.
I disobeyed and caused this wind."

Still, the mariners all sailed,
but the waves and wind prevailed.

So *splash!*
they threw Jonah in.
And it ceased—
that mighty wind!

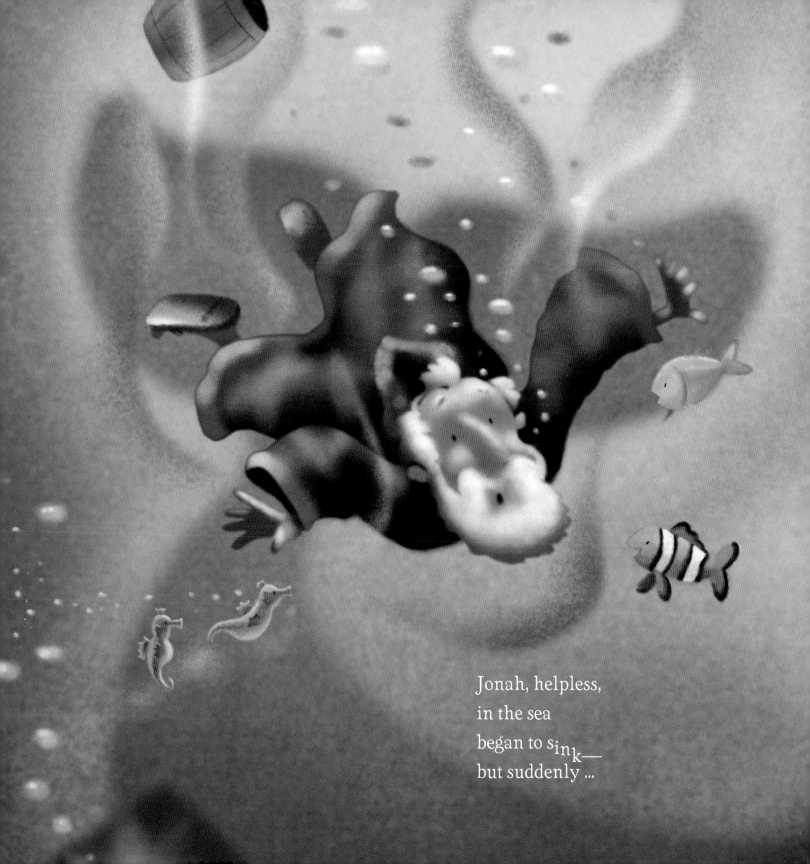

Jonah, helpless,
in the sea
began to s$_{in}$$_k$—
but suddenly ...

A great big fish
opened W-I-D-E,
swallowed Jonah
deep inside.

Down
and
down
and
down
he went,
cold and
frightened,
wet and spent.

It was dark,
damp, and dreary.
Jonah, troubled and
so weary,

oh, was sorry
he had fled.
Should have done
what God had said.

In that belly day and night,
Jonah prayed ... with all his might.

Three long days—finally ...

God heard Jonah's mournful plea.

Made that fish
swim to land,
spit him out upon the sand,

where once again ...

Jonah heard the Lord's command.

"Go to Nineveh,"
I say.
Jonah said,
"I will obey."

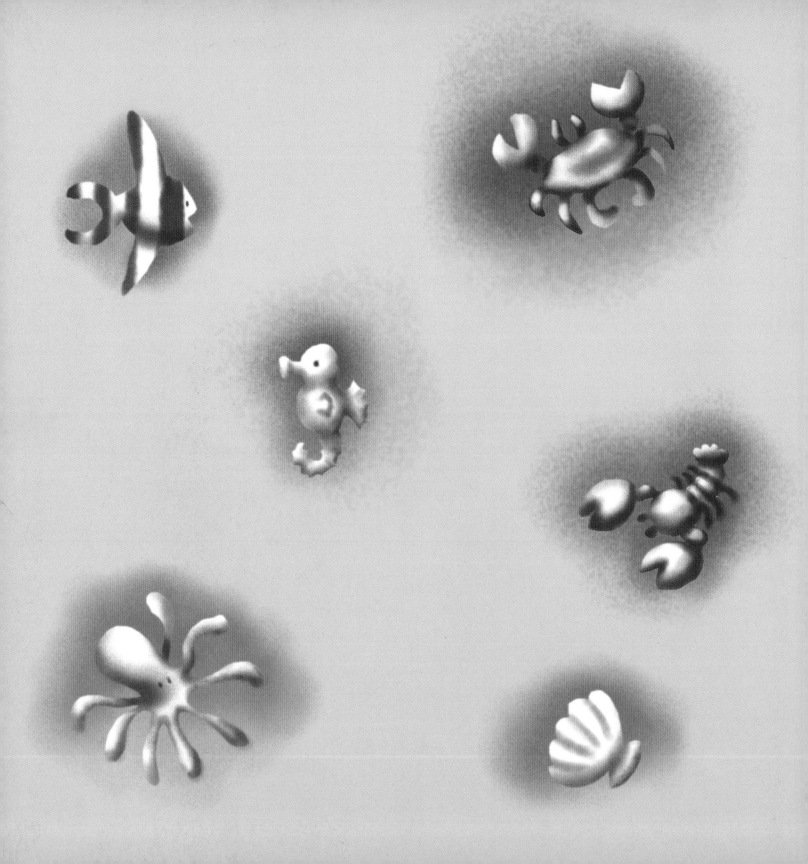